Zodiac Signs

LIBRA

DiscoverRoo
An Imprint of Pop!
popbooksonline.com

by Elizabeth Andrews

WELCOME TO DiscoverRoo!

This book is filled with videos, puzzles, games, and more! Scan the QR codes* while you read, or visit the website below to make this book pop.

popbooksonline.com/libra

abdobooks.com

Published by Pop!, a division of ABDO, PO Box 398166, Minneapolis, Minnesota 55439.

Printed in the United States of America, North Mankato, Minnesota.

042025
082025

THIS BOOK CONTAINS RECYCLED MATERIALS

Cover Photo: Splendoura Prints; Shutterstock Images
Interior Photos: Getty Images; Shutterstock Images
Editor: Tyler Gieseke
Series Designer: Laura Graphenteen

Library of Congress Control Number: 2024948388

Publisher's Cataloging-in-Publication Data

Names: Andrews, Elizabeth, author.
Title: Libra / by Elizabeth Andrews
Description: Minneapolis, Minnesota : Pop!, 2026 | Series: Zodiac signs | Includes online resources and index
Identifiers: ISBN 9781098247928 (lib. bdg.) | ISBN 9781098248468 (ebook)
Subjects: LCSH: Libra (Astrology)--Juvenile literature. | Balance (Astrology)--Juvenile literature. | Scales (Astrology)--Juvenile literature. | Zodiac--Juvenile literature. | Astrology--Juvenile literature. | Astrology--Charts, diagrams, etc.--Juvenile literature.
Classification: DDC 133.52--dc23

*Scanning QR codes requires a web-enabled smart device with a QR code reader app and a camera.

TABLE OF CONTENTS

CHAPTER 1

MEET THE LIBRA!

Libra is the seventh sign of the zodiac. Libras are born between September 23 and October 23. When people ask for your "star sign," they are likely asking for your sun sign. This is the zodiac sign the sun appeared in at your birth.

WATCH A VIDEO HERE!

Rose

September 23–October 23

LIBRA

ZODIAC CALENDAR

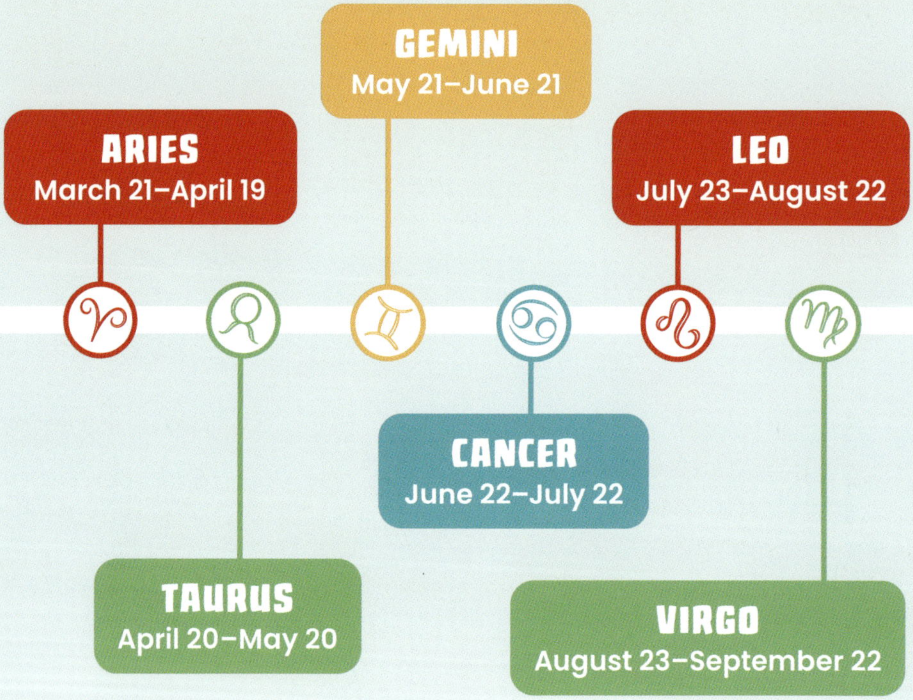

Three features help describe zodiac signs. Signs can be masculine or feminine. Each zodiac sign is given a mode. The three modes are cardinal, fixed, and mutable. Each zodiac is also

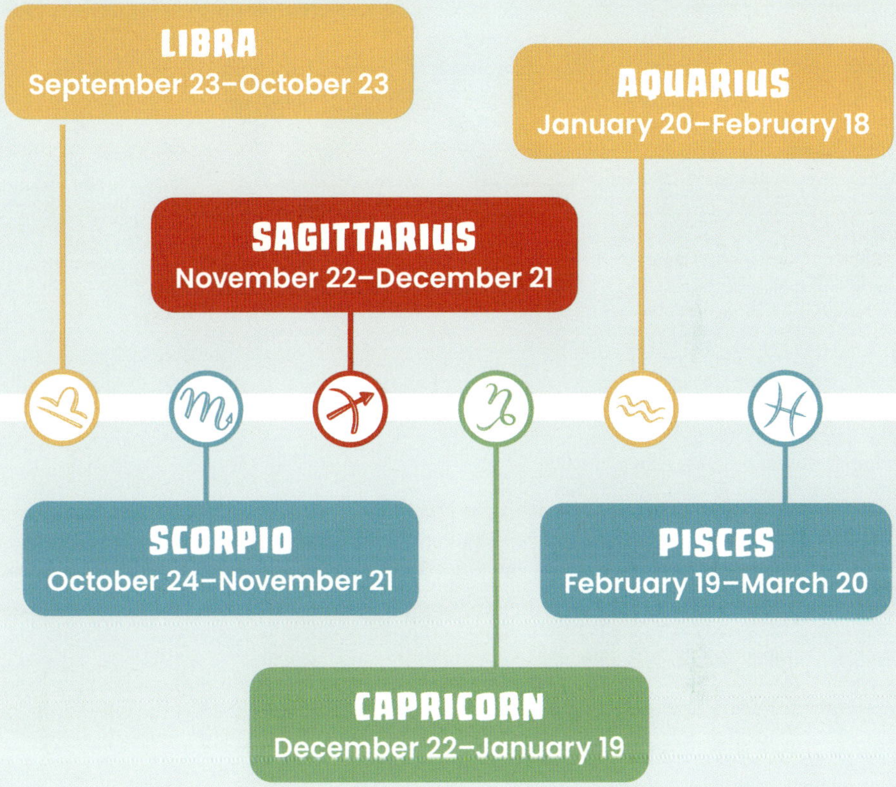

a fire, air, earth, or water sign. No zodiac sign shares the same three features.

DID YOU KNOW?

Libras get along best with air and fire signs.

Libras are happiest when they are with their friends.

Libra is a masculine, cardinal, air sign. People with masculine signs are reasonable and action focused. They usually say exactly what they mean. They are outgoing and strong.

Modes determine how signs interact with the outside world. Cardinal signs make things happen. They are quick to act when an idea strikes. Air signs are smart and talkative. They are often curious and quirky.

Cardinal signs are born in the beginning of seasons. They are often leaders.

Libras are **represented** by the scales. The scales were the ancient **symbol** of fairness, balance, and order. Some people believe the sun passed in front of the Libra **constellation** on the autumnal equinox. This is when day and night are equal in length. They are in balance. Greeks believed Libra was the claws of the Scorpius constellation.

The Libra constellation can be seen best in late June.

The Greek goddess of fairness was called Themis. Her symbol was the scales.

CHAPTER 2

HISTORY OF ASTROLOGY

Humans have looked for life's **spiritual** meaning since the beginning of time. They often looked to the stars for this. Astrology is the practice of reading the movements of planets and other **celestial** bodies and connecting them to life on Earth.

LEARN MORE HERE!

Some ancient people used the zodiac signs to predict future events.

Babylonians invented the zodiac in Mesopotamia over 5,000 years ago. Mesopotamia was the first known civilization. Babylon was one of the region's largest cities.

Ptolemy was an Egyptian man who studied the stars.

Earth and our solar system are in the Milky Way galaxy.

The zodiac is a belt of space around Earth that has 12 well-known **constellations**. Ancient people noticed that the sun seemed to move in front of these constellations throughout a year. The sun spends about a month in each constellation.

The constellations in the zodiac belt are Aries, Taurus, Gemini, Cancer, Leo, Virgo, Libra, Scorpius, Sagittarius, Capricornus, Aquarius, and Pisces. Together they make up the 12 zodiac signs. They are all **represented** by different **symbols**.

Islamic astrologers created new ways to map and measure stars.

THE ZODIAC WHEEL

DID YOU KNOW?

Most zodiac signs are animals. The ancient Greeks called the belt of space *zodiakos kyklos,* or "circle of animals."

CHAPTER 3

SIGN OF PARTNERSHIPS

Libra is ruled by the planet Venus. Venus is the Roman goddess of love, beauty, pleasure, emotions, and art. Libras like to show beauty to others in how they look and in their homes. They are known to have good taste. Libras are loving people. They are often warmhearted.

EXPLORE LINKS HERE!

Actor Jenna Ortega is a Libra. She was born on September 27, 2002.

Young Libras often take time to help their community.

Since Libras are born under the scales, they want balance in all things. They are concerned with fairness and equality for the people close to them and the world. Sometimes, their commitment to fairness makes them seem **stubborn**. But they just want equality for all.

Libras are very easygoing. They hate to upset anyone or rock the boat. They go out of their way to avoid disagreements and arguments. Libras are good people to have around during disagreements between others though. Libras are calm and hear all points of view in arguments. They will stand up for people who are being treated unfairly.

Libras enjoy people who are easygoing like them.

Libras always want to make their loved ones proud.

Libra is the sign of partnerships. Partnerships are relationships based on shared goals. Libras feel best while sharing their ideas, time, and emotions with others. Partnerships give them a purpose. Luckily, people are very drawn to Libras. People enjoy Libras' warm spirit and positive energy.

DID YOU KNOW?

Libra partnerships can be with romantic partners, family members, coworkers, or friends.

CHAPTER 4

THE CHARMER

Libras have a gift of making other people feel important just by being with them. They are great listeners. Libras' personalities change based on whom they are with. Since they are such good

COMPLETE AN ACTIVITY HERE!

Opals display all colors of the rainbow.

To be charming means to easily attract people and make them happy.

listeners, they know how to please those they are around. This connects to their wish to keep the peace.

DID YOU KNOW?

Sometimes, Libras feel like they are using their charm to trick people into liking them.

DON'T BE FOOLED

Libras can often be fooled by people who appear warm and charming like themselves. As a sign ruled by Venus, Libras won't look much deeper than a beautiful outer shell.

Libras often push aside their own needs. Sometimes, they don't know their true feelings because they are so focused on the feelings of others.

Libras want other people to like them. They struggle saying "no" when people ask them for help. Libras need to give to themselves as much as they give to others.

Mahatma Gandhi was a Libra. He fought peacefully for social justice in India.

Libras often care deeply about tradition and their family history.

School counselors offer help and advice to students.

At work, Libras are great team players. They connect with the people they work with. Libras make good **social justice lawyers** or counselors. As a sign ruled by Venus, Libras also do well in jobs in the arts. However, because they are so easygoing, they might have trouble completing tasks.

Today, astrology can answer questions about an individual. People use astrology to understand who they are and why they might do what they do. It can also help them understand other people in their life. A zodiac sign can point out personal skills, possibilities, and **internal motivations**.

WHAT IS A BIRTH CHART?

Each person's birth chart contains all the planets in our solar system, the moon, and the sun. The location of where each **celestial** body was based on the exact time and location of a person's birth can be marked on a birth chart. A birth chart can explain even more about a person than what only a sun sign can. The placement of each planet affects the drive of a person. This reveals personal motivations. Astrology experts can read birth charts.

MAKING CONNECTIONS

TEXT-TO-SELF

Are you a Libra? If so, do you think the sign matches your personality? If not, what do you have in common with Libras?

TEXT-TO-TEXT

Have you read any books about the other zodiac signs? How were those signs similar to and different from Libras?

TEXT-TO-WORLD

With the help of an adult, look up famous Libras. Pick one person and write a few sentences about ways that person shows Libra qualities.

GLOSSARY

celestial — having to do with the sky or outer space.

constellation — a group of stars that forms a pattern.

internal — of, relating to, or being on the inside.

lawyer — one whose job is to help people with legal matters and represent them in court.

motivation — something that makes one want to do something.

represent — to stand for or be a sign of.

social justice — the belief that all people should have equal rights and opportunities.

spiritual — having to do with people's beliefs in things such as the soul, nature, and what happens after death.

stubborn — not willing to accept change.

symbol — an object or picture that represents something else.

INDEX